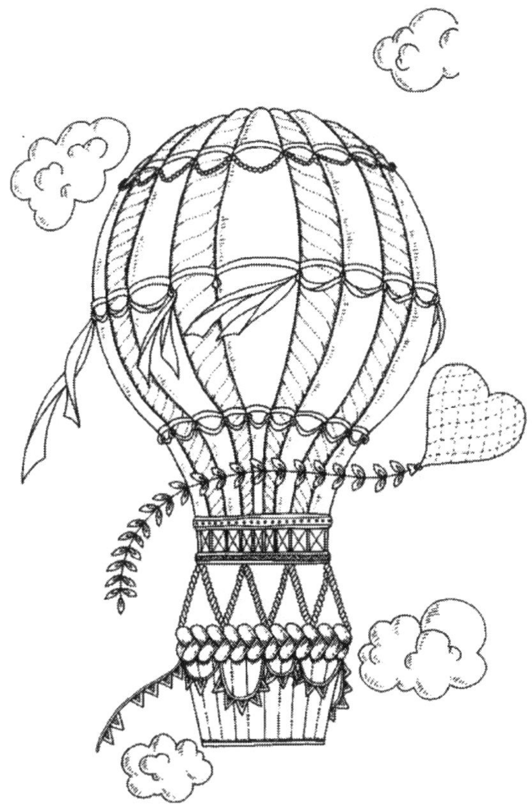

BALLOON PUBLISHING

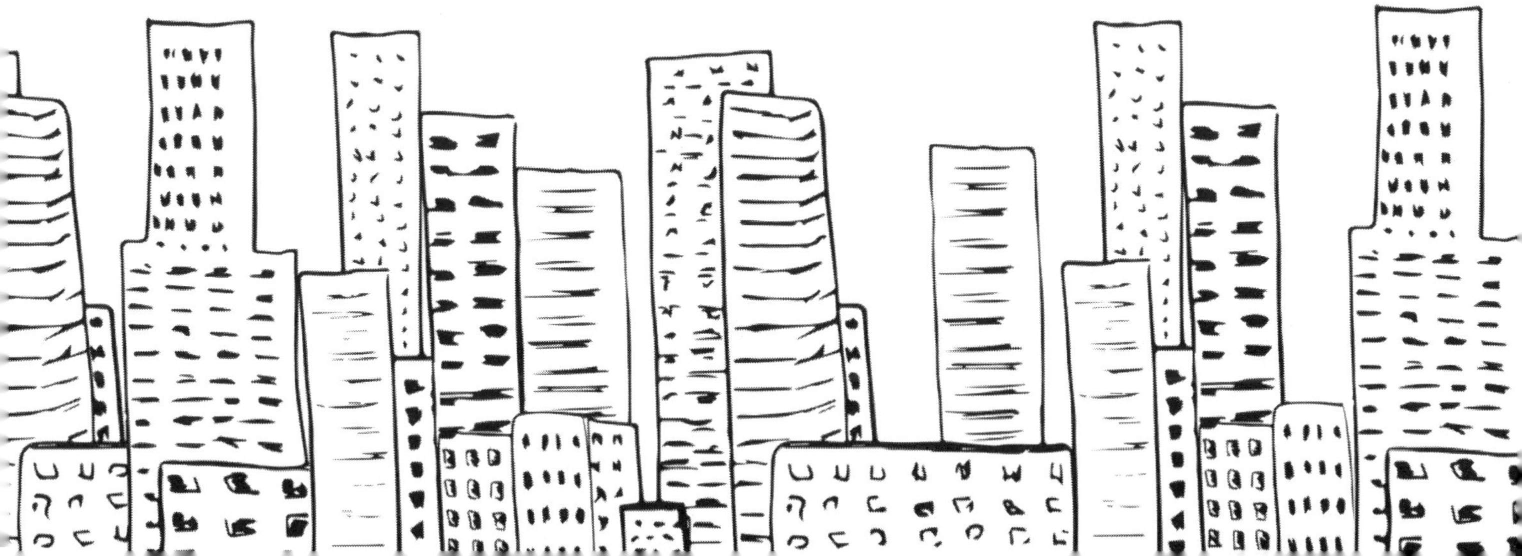

FREE DOWNLOAD

www.balloonpublishing.com/freedownload

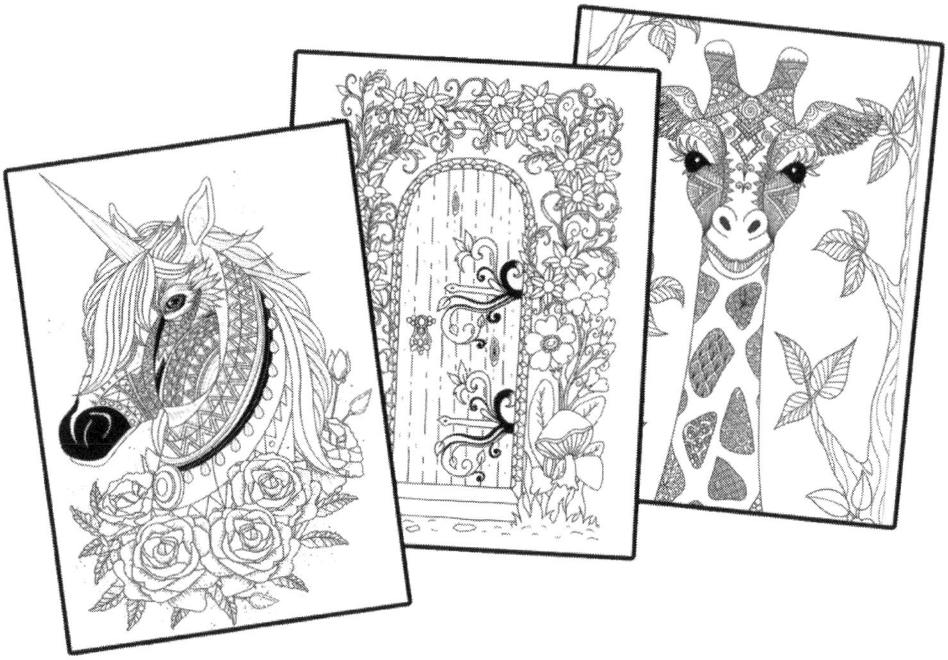

Balloon Publishing

@balloonpublishing

COLOR TEST PAGE

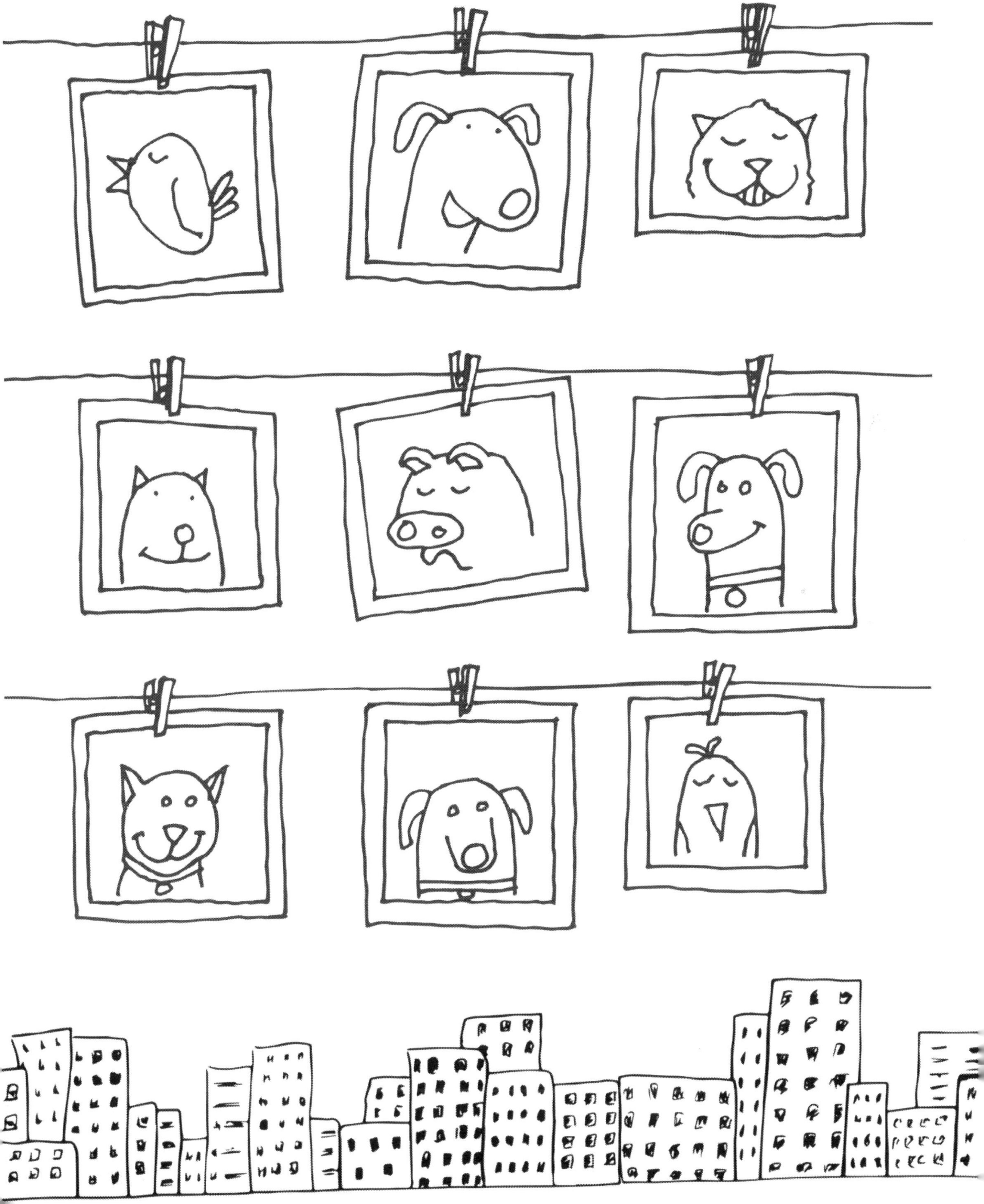

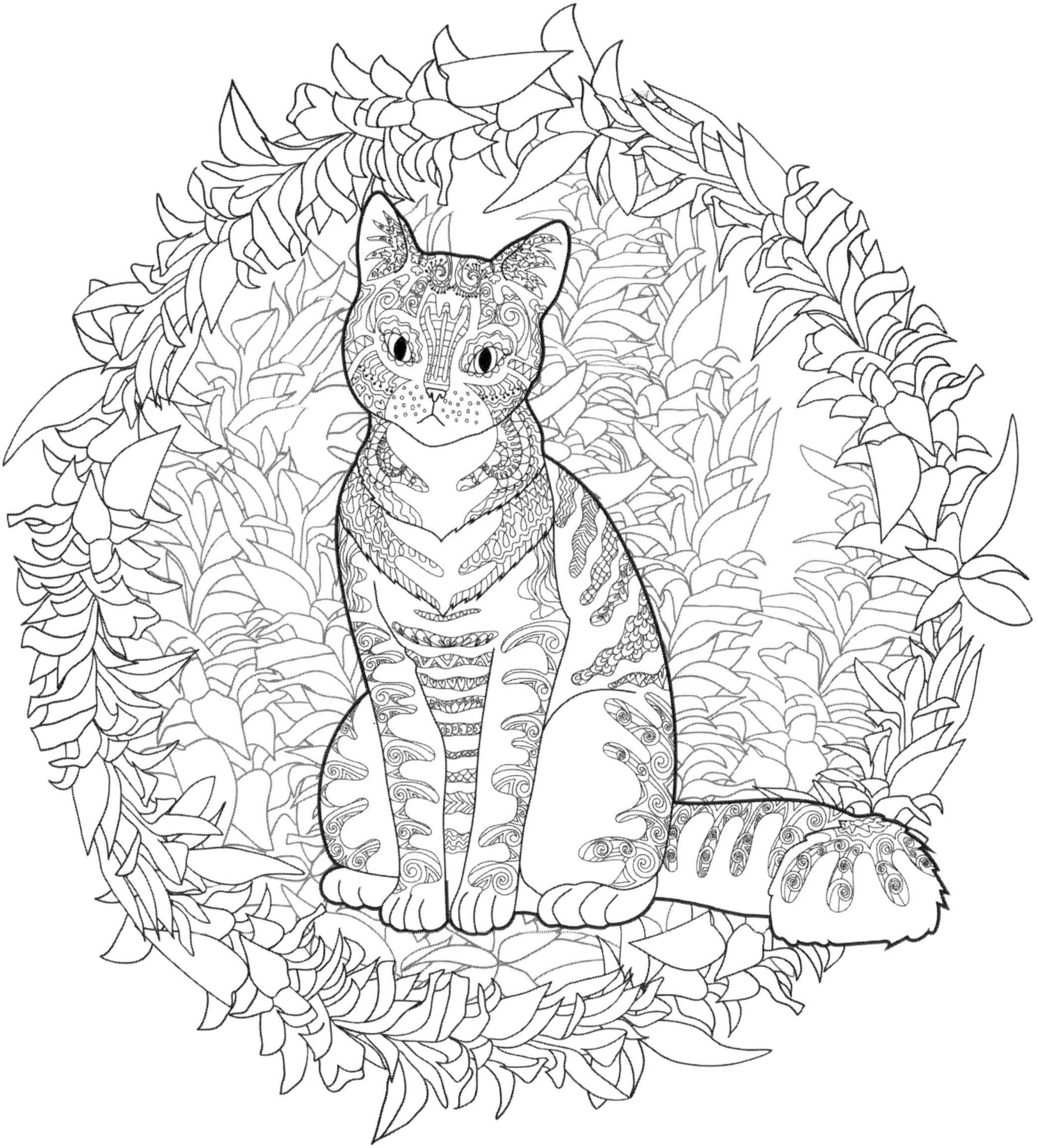

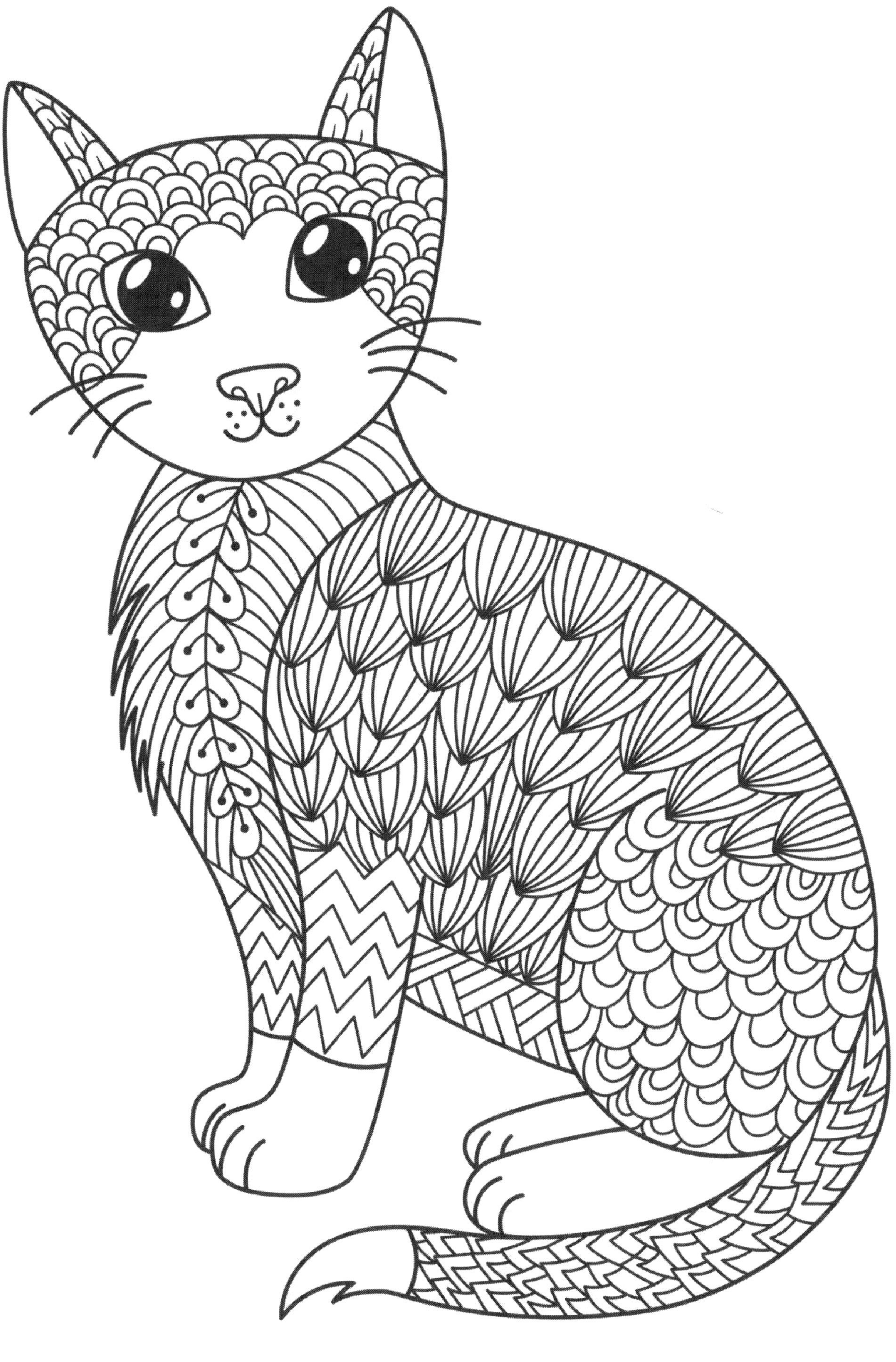

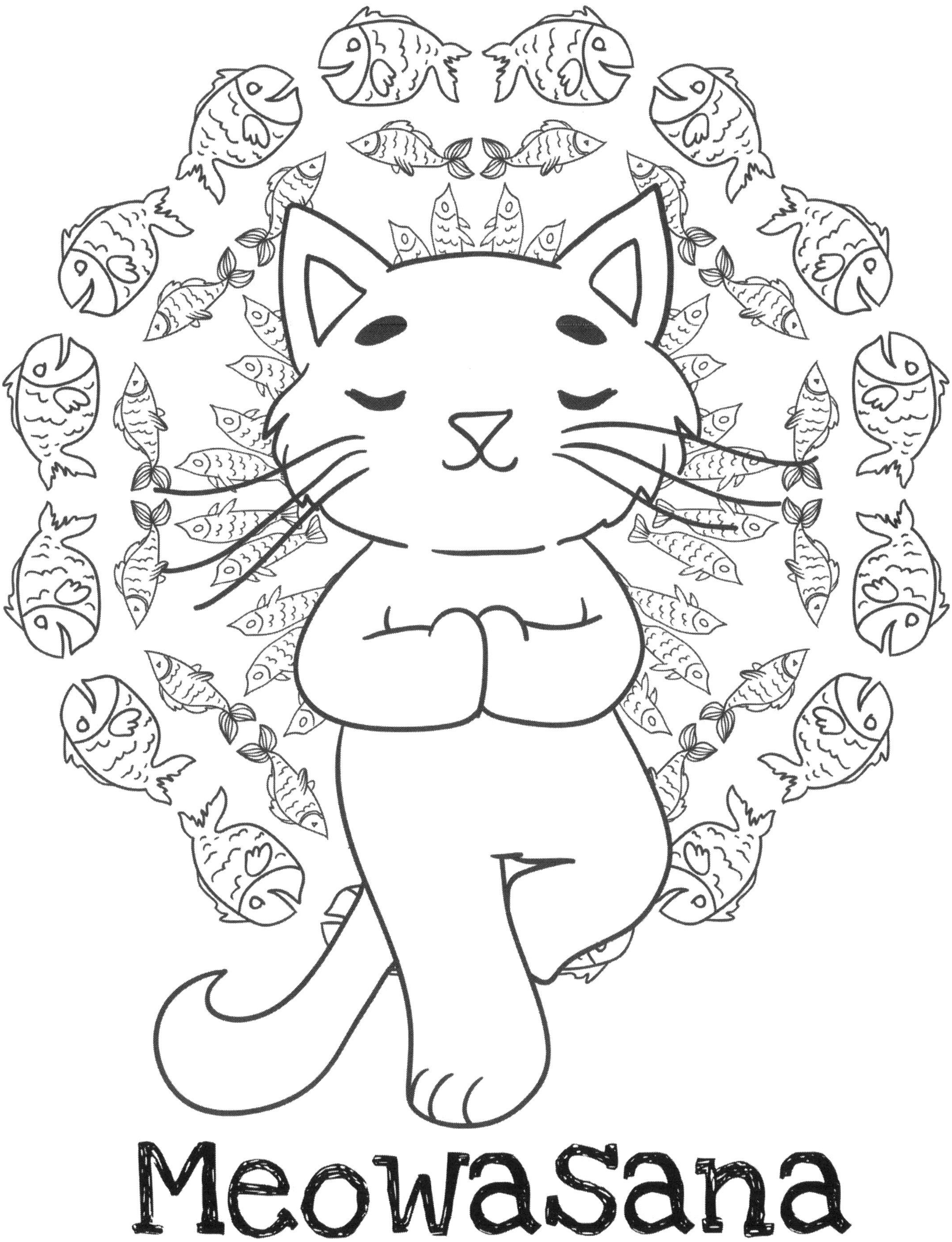

Meowasana

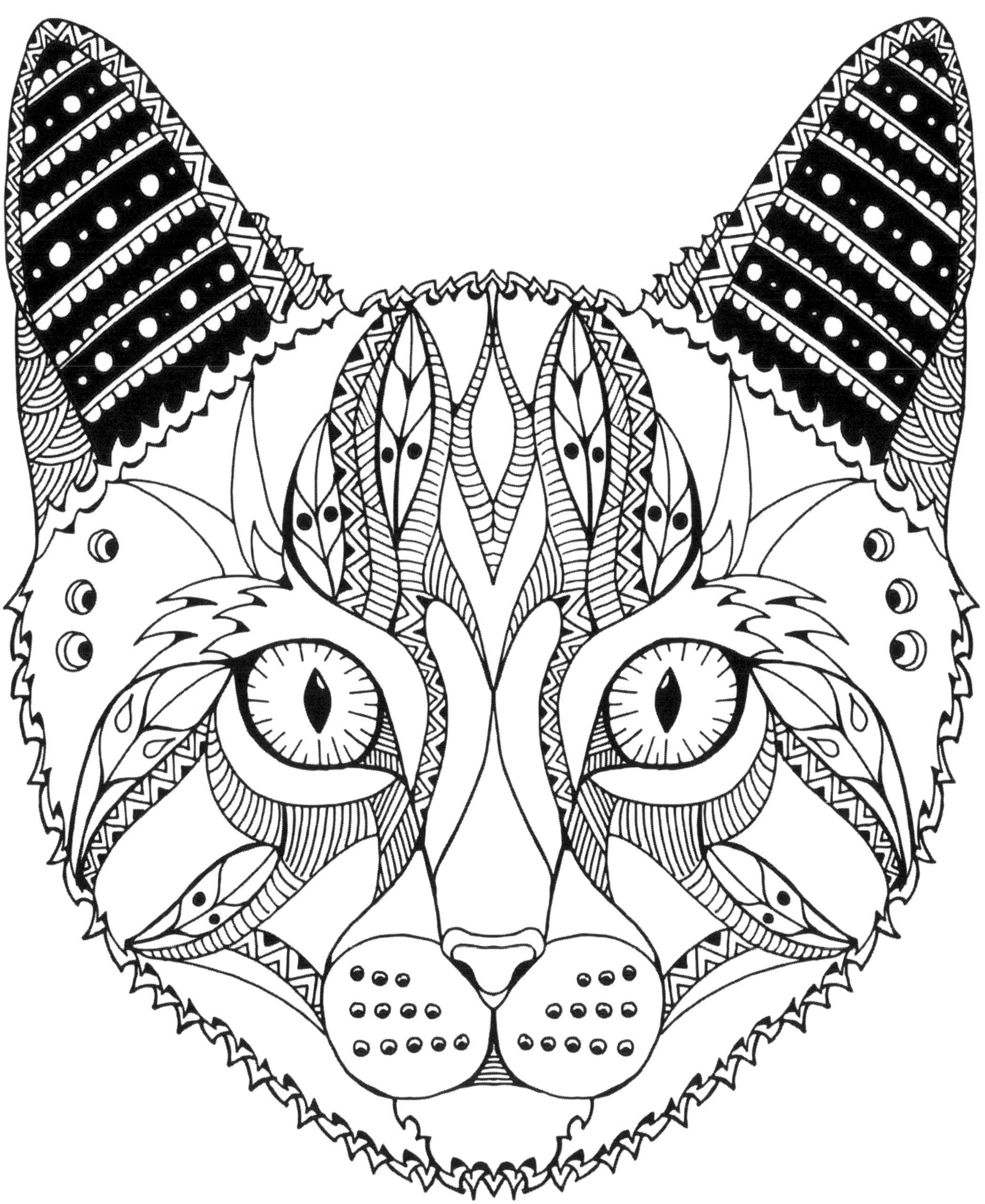

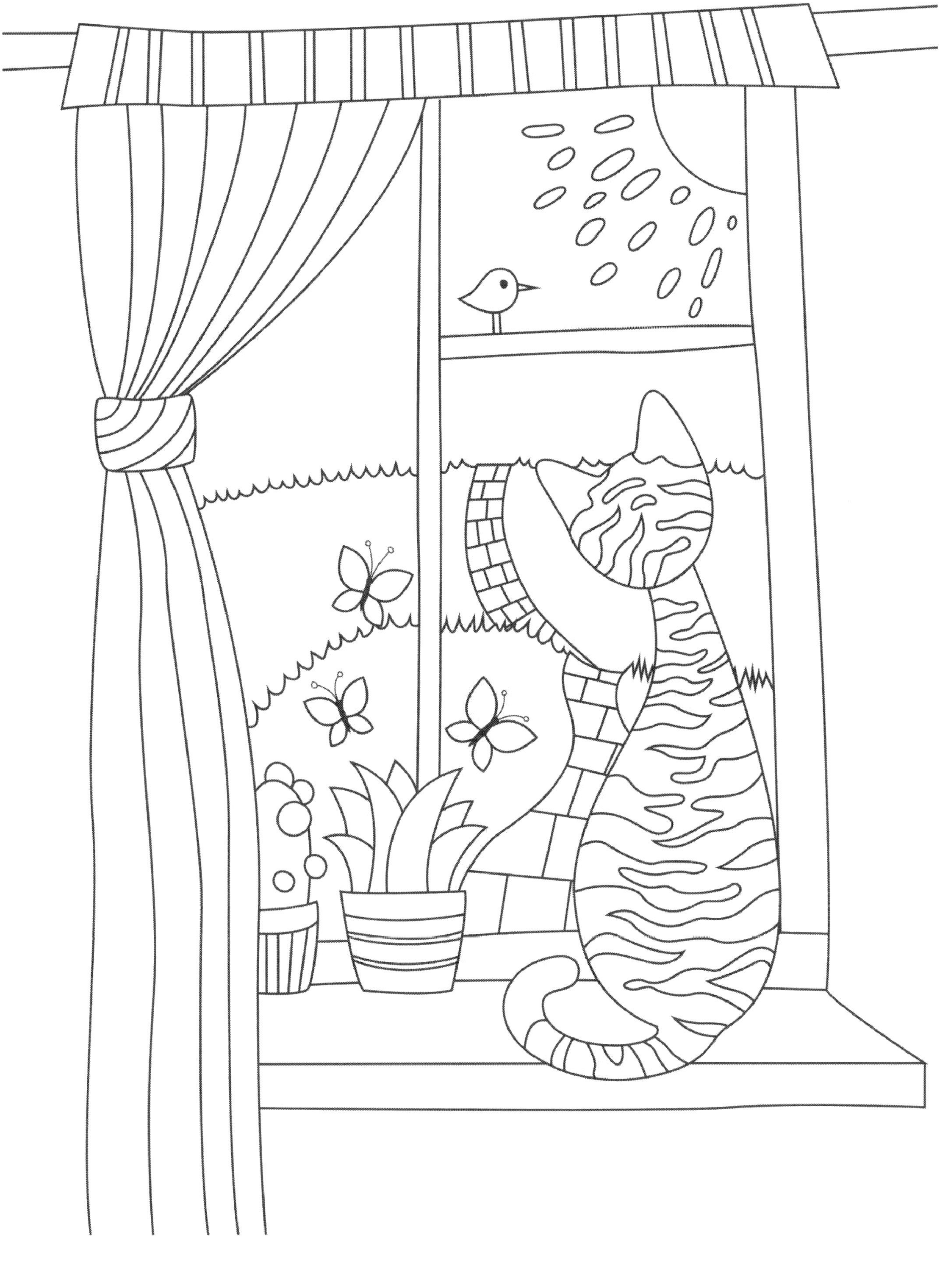

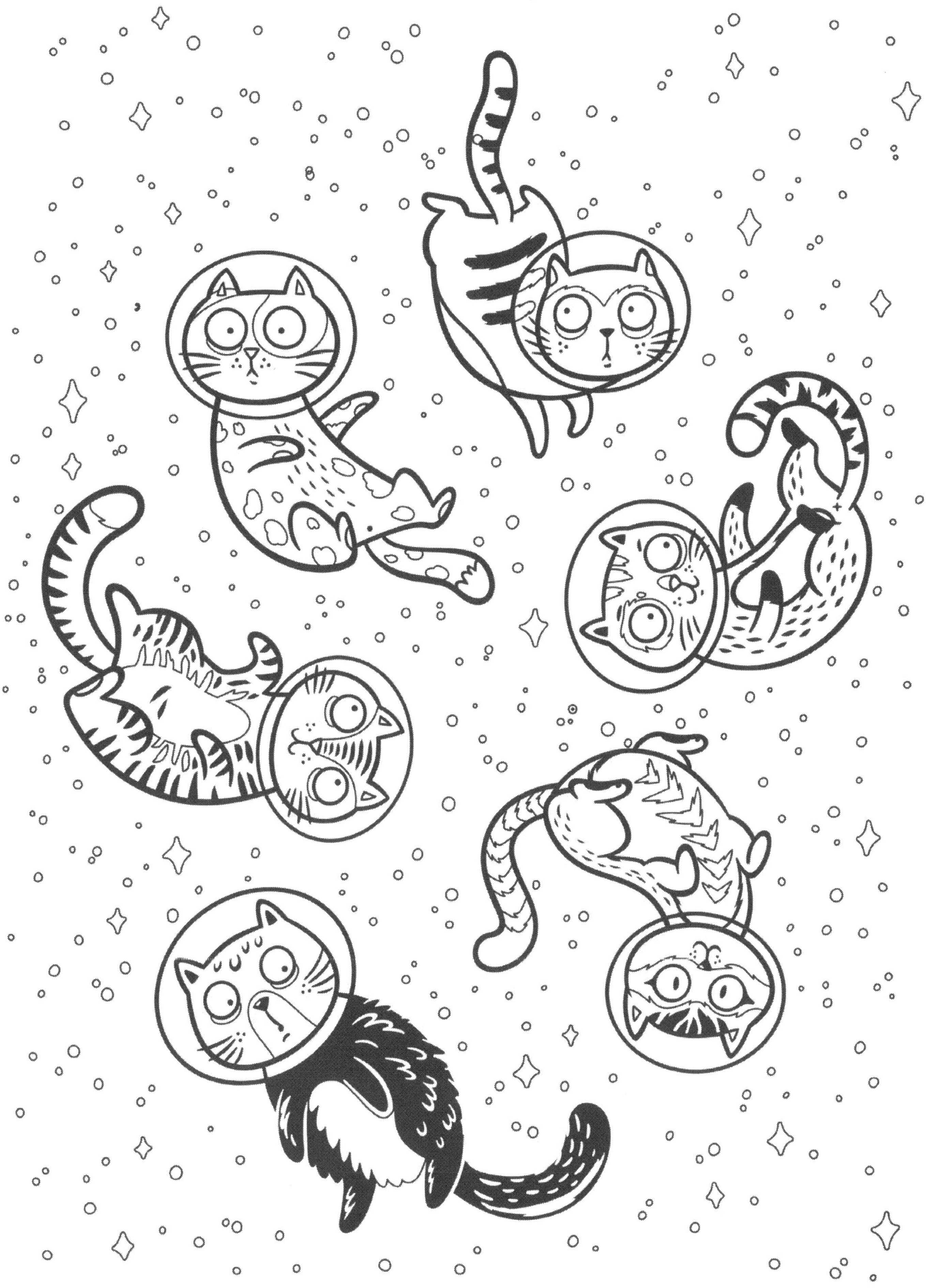

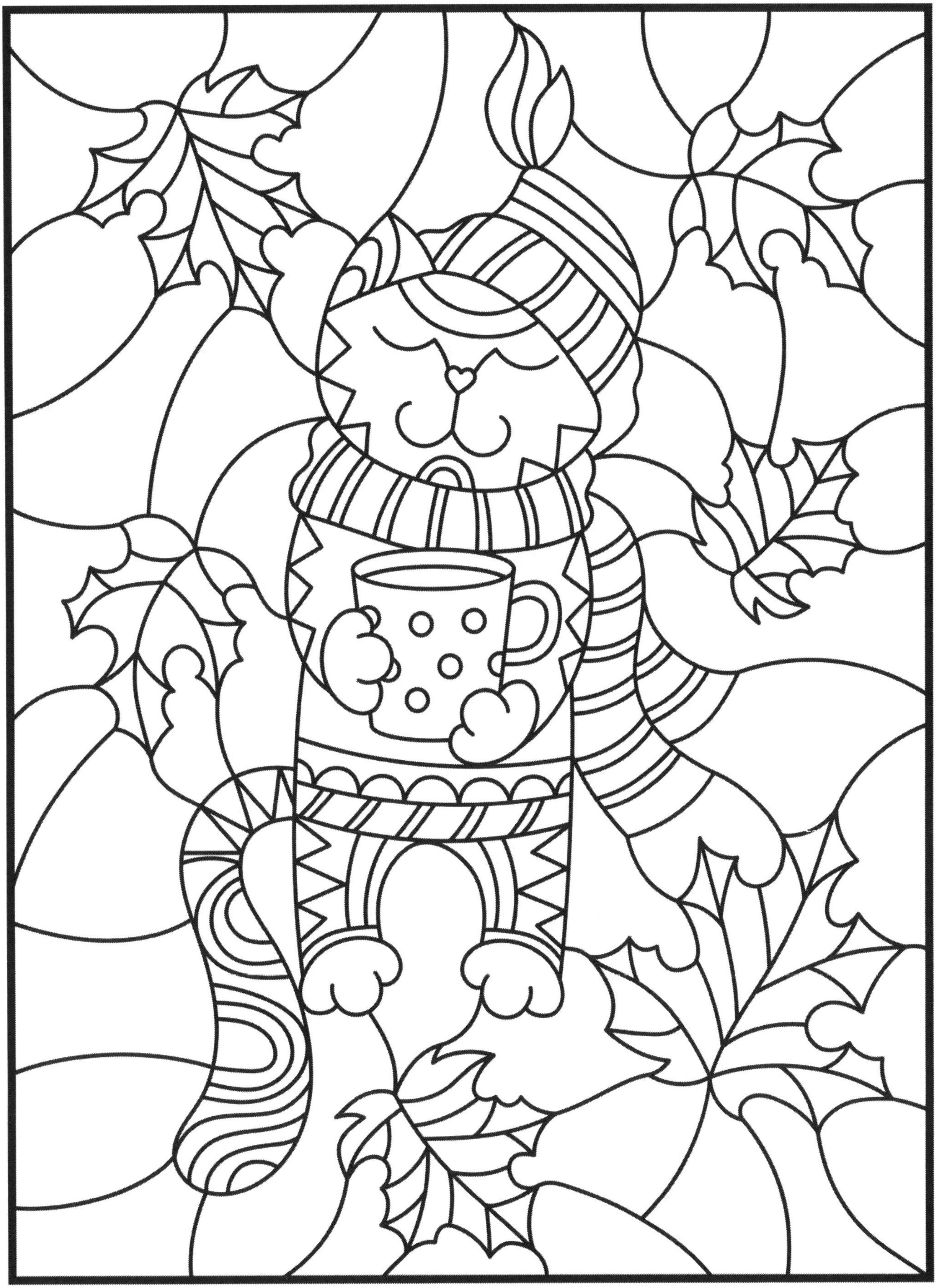

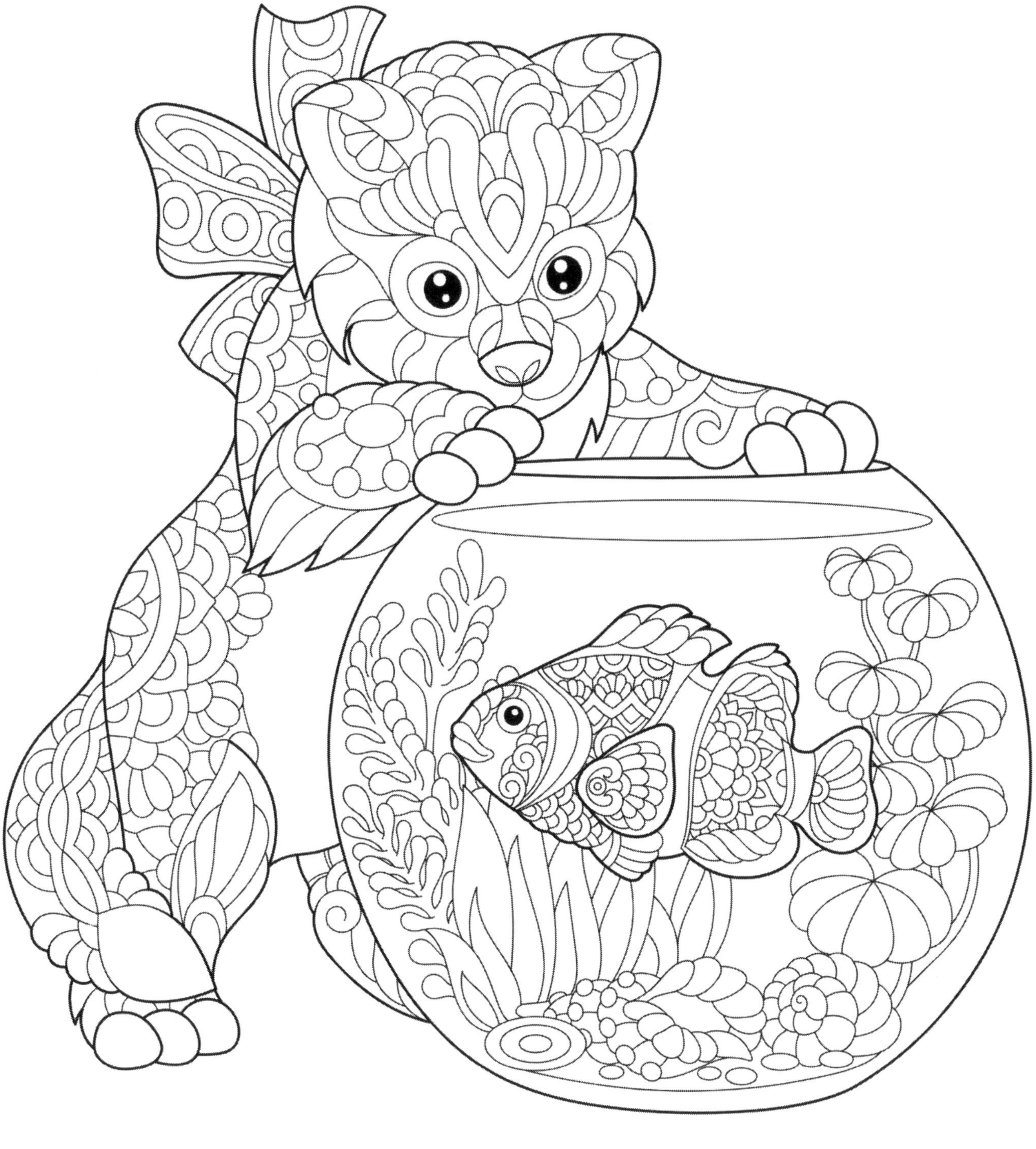

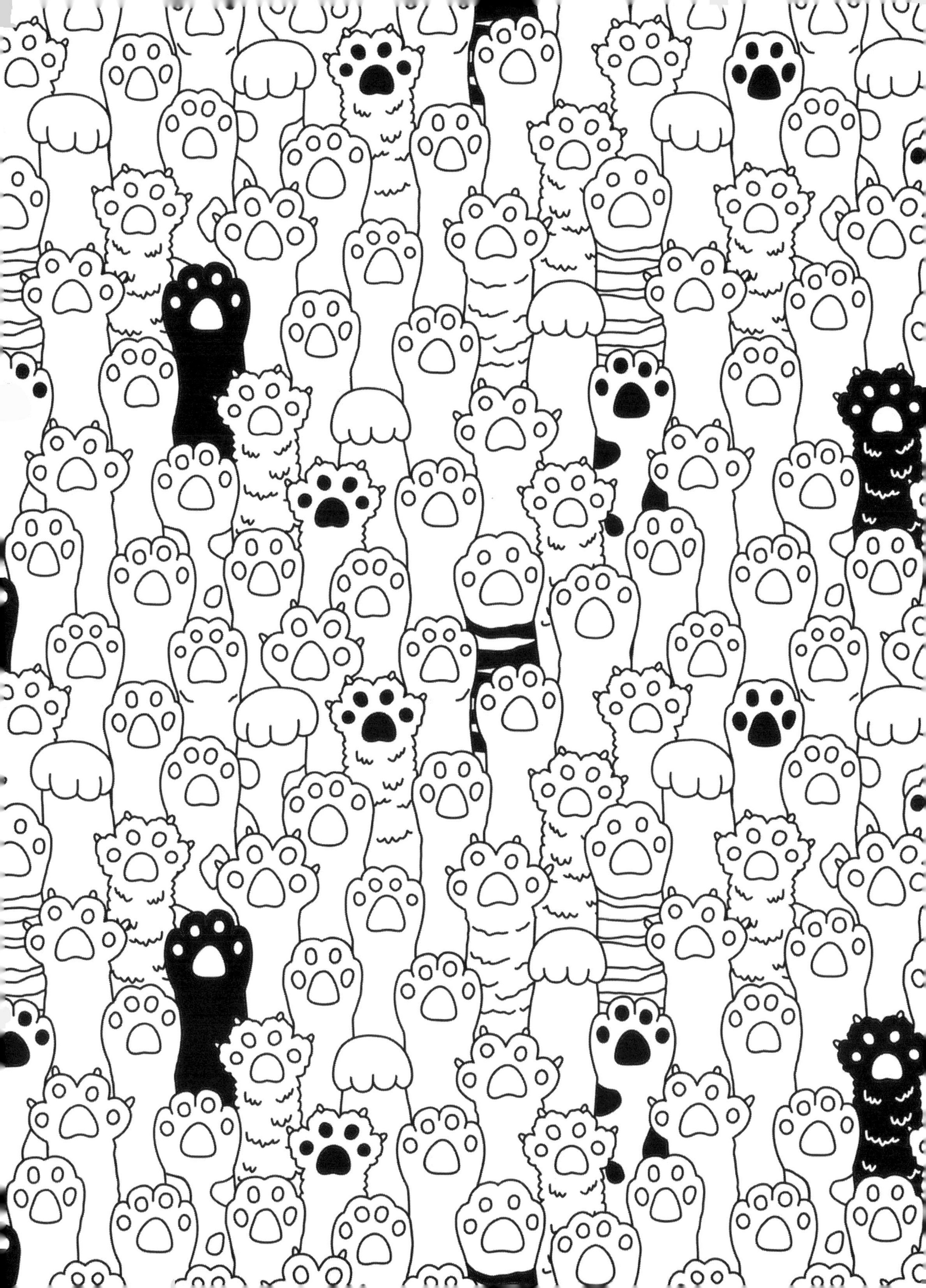

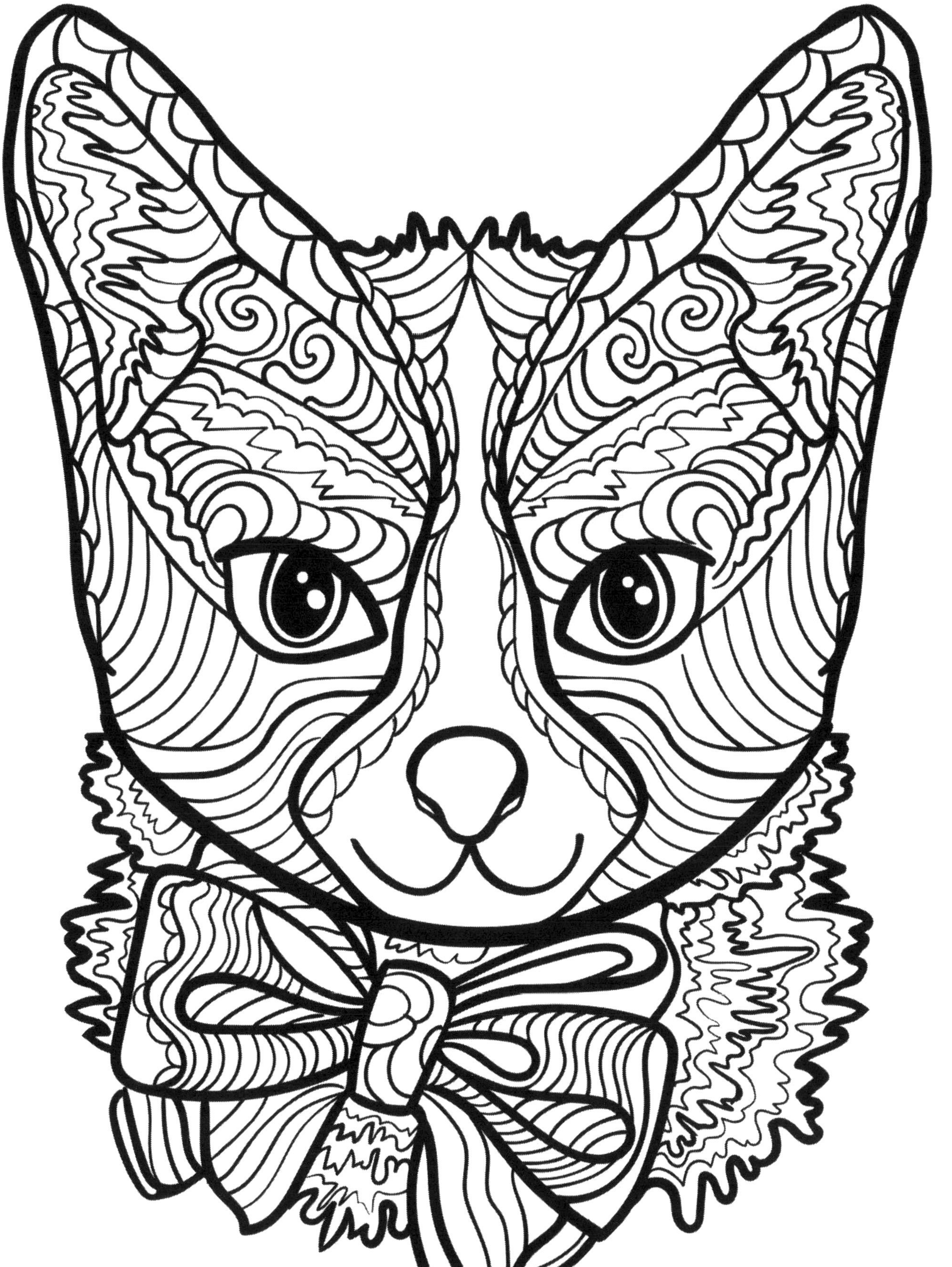

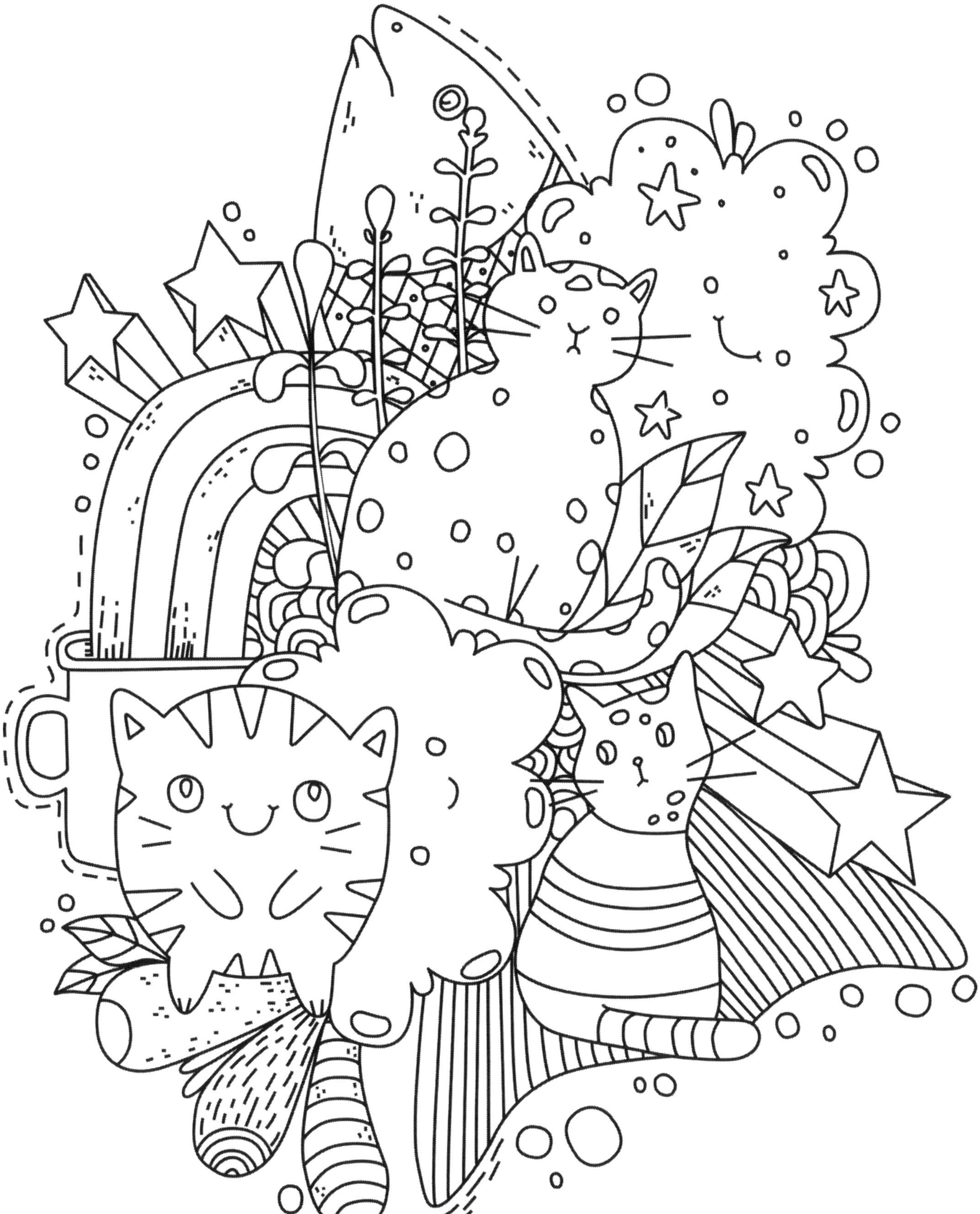

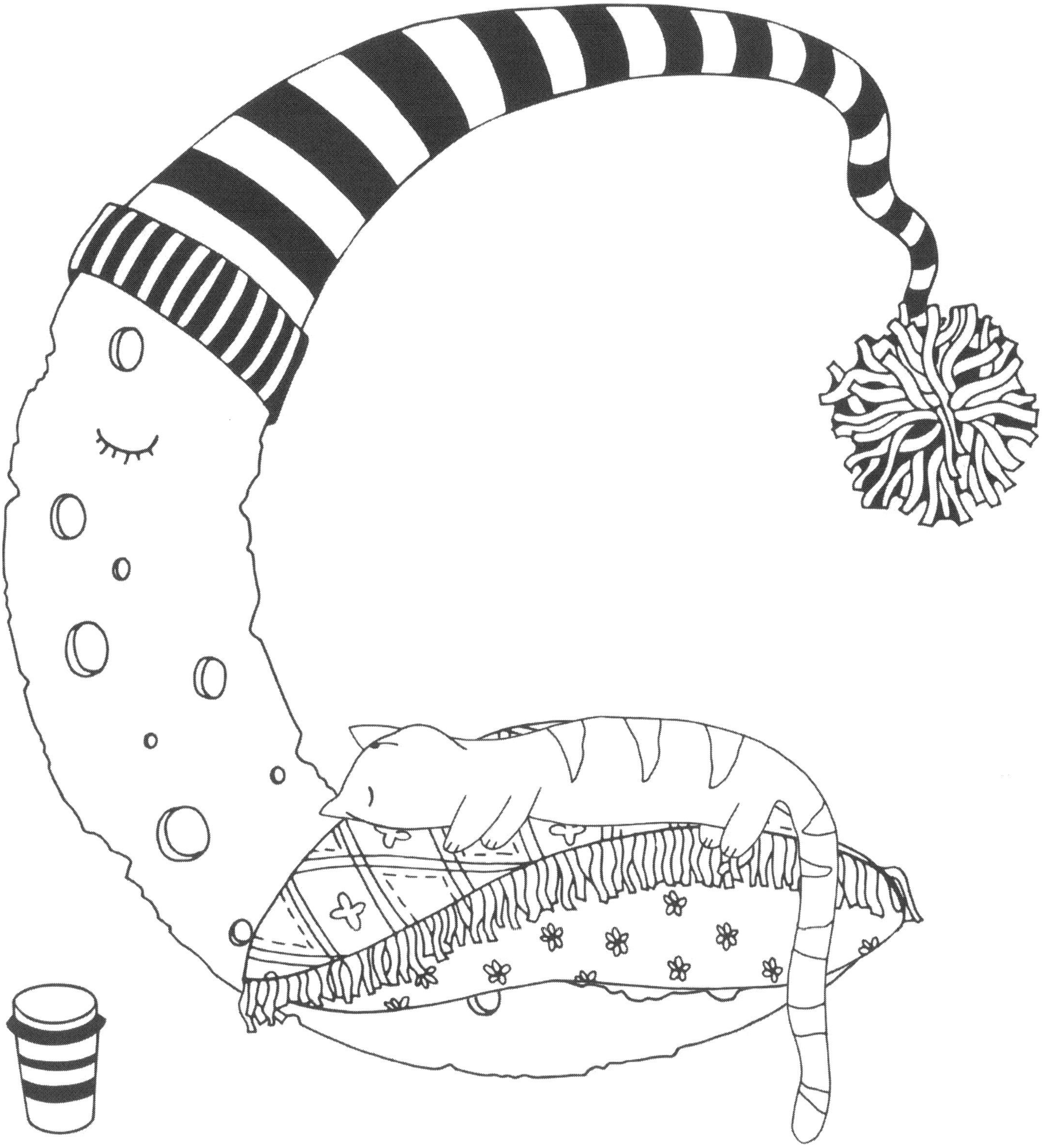

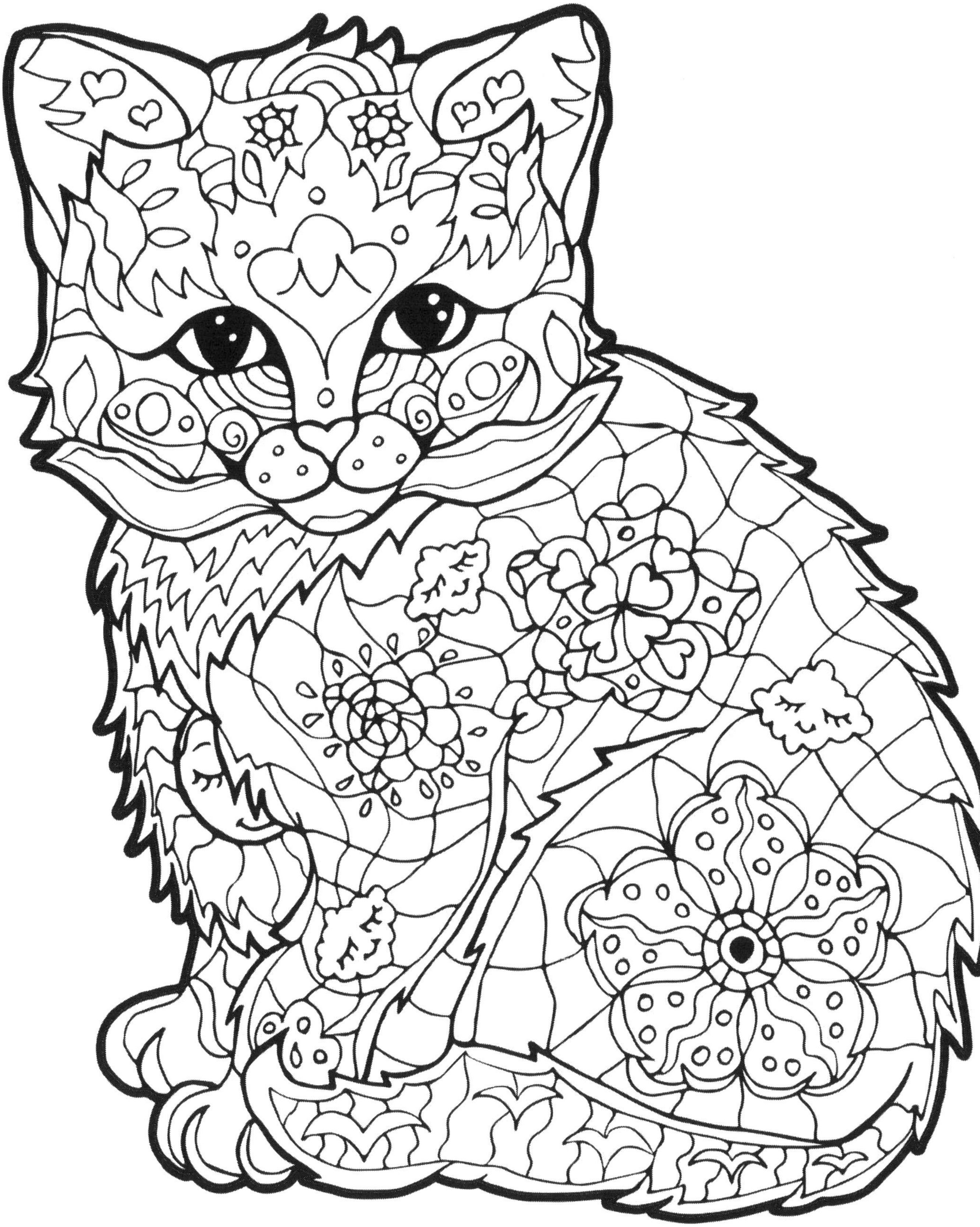

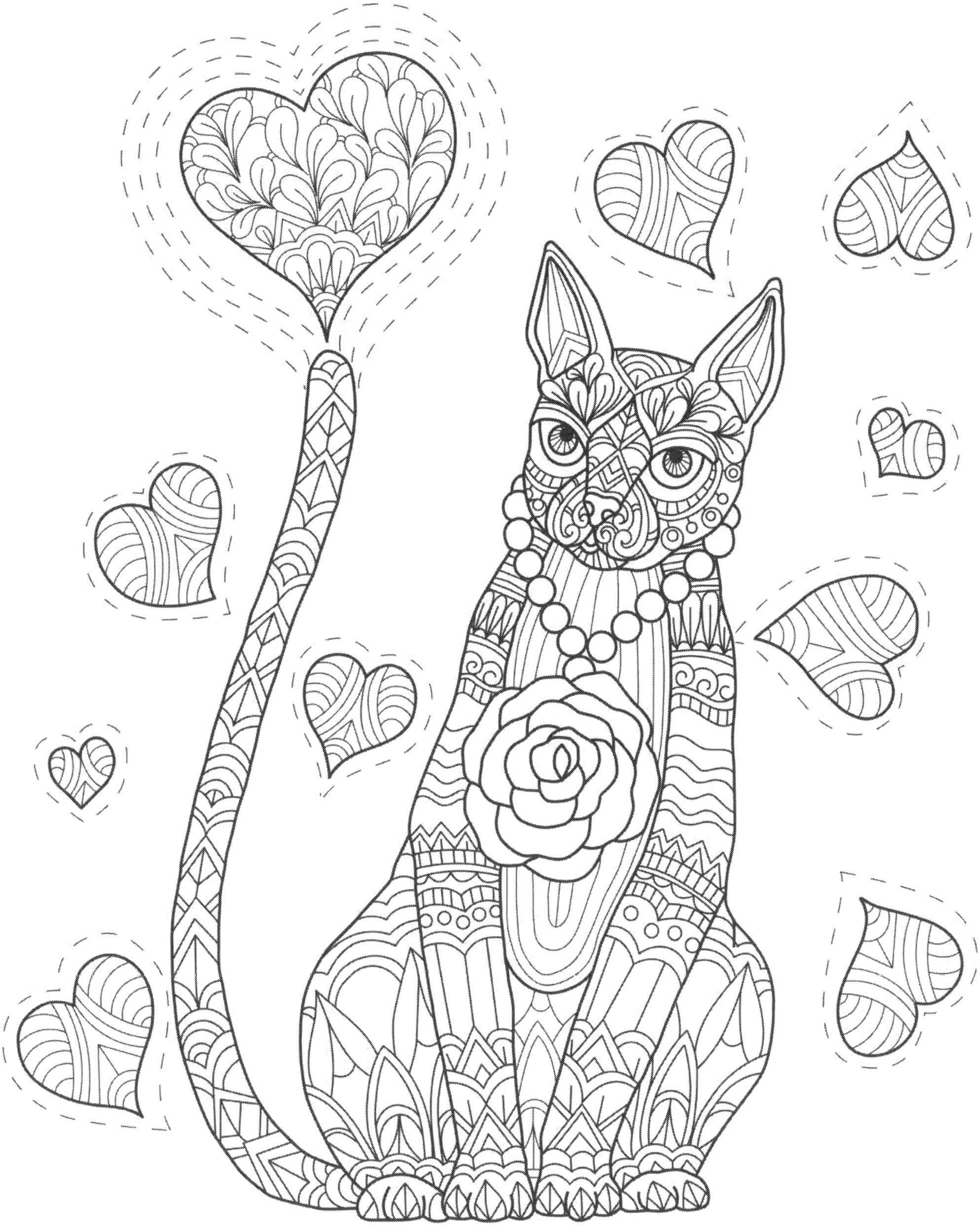

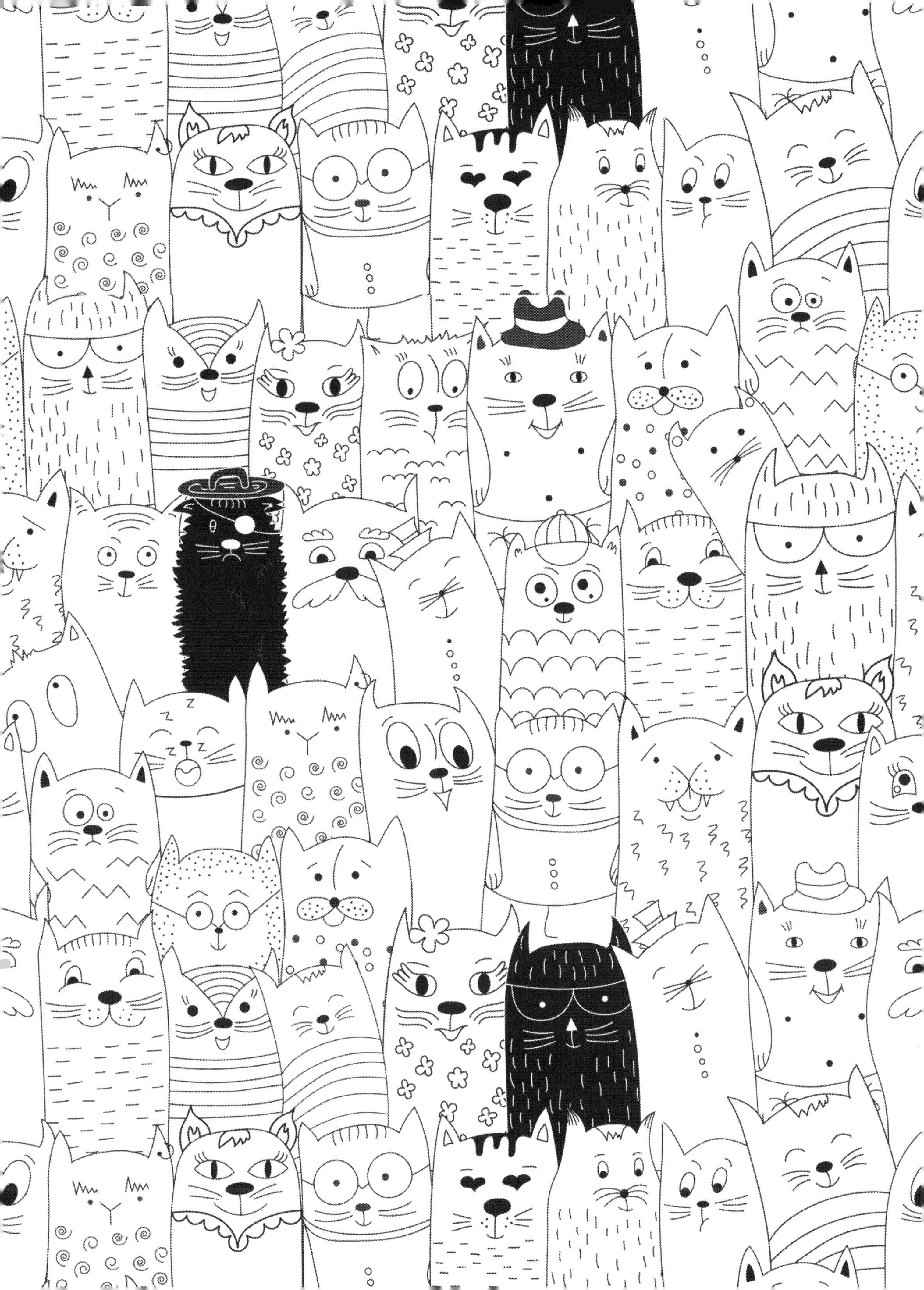

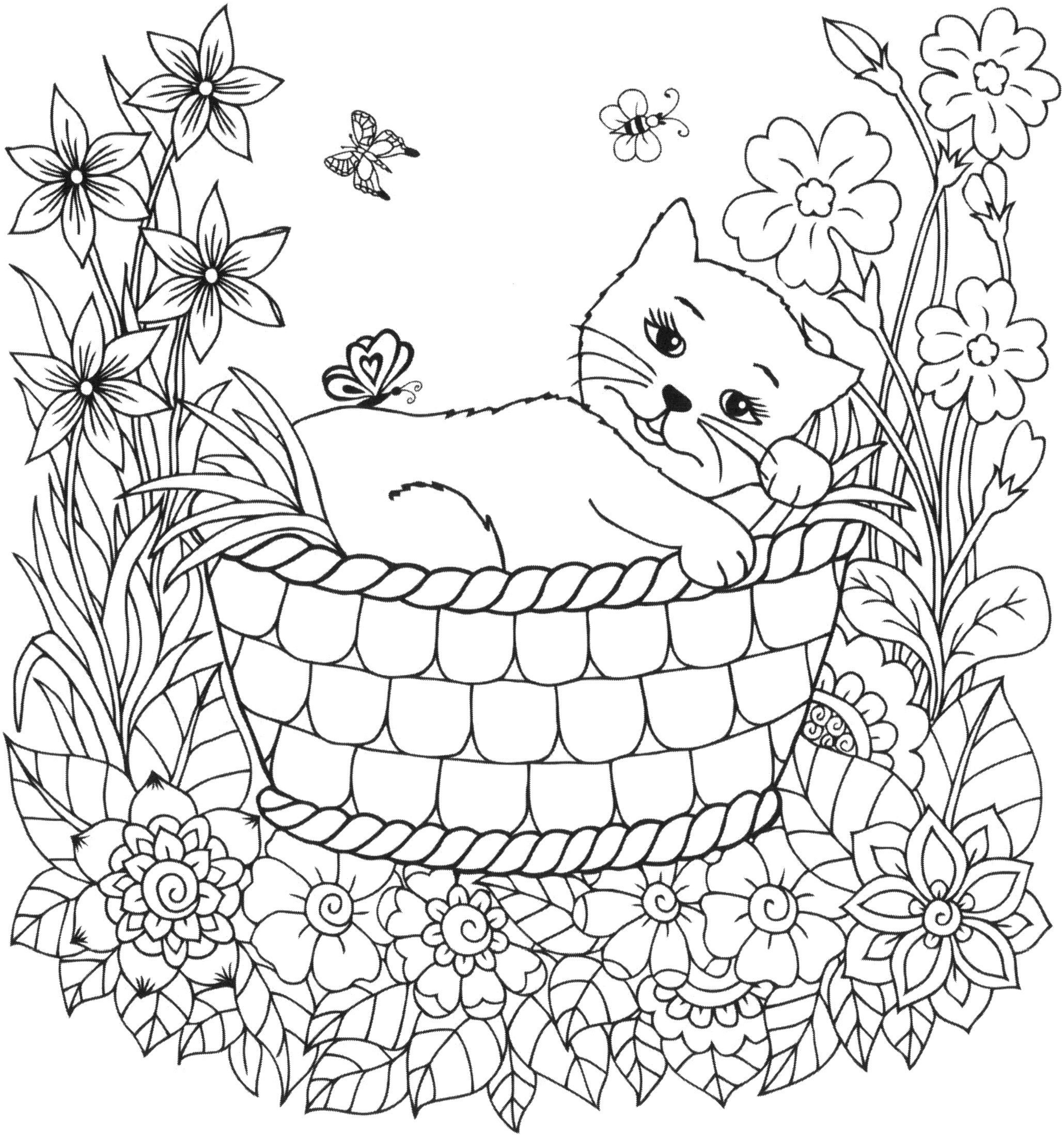

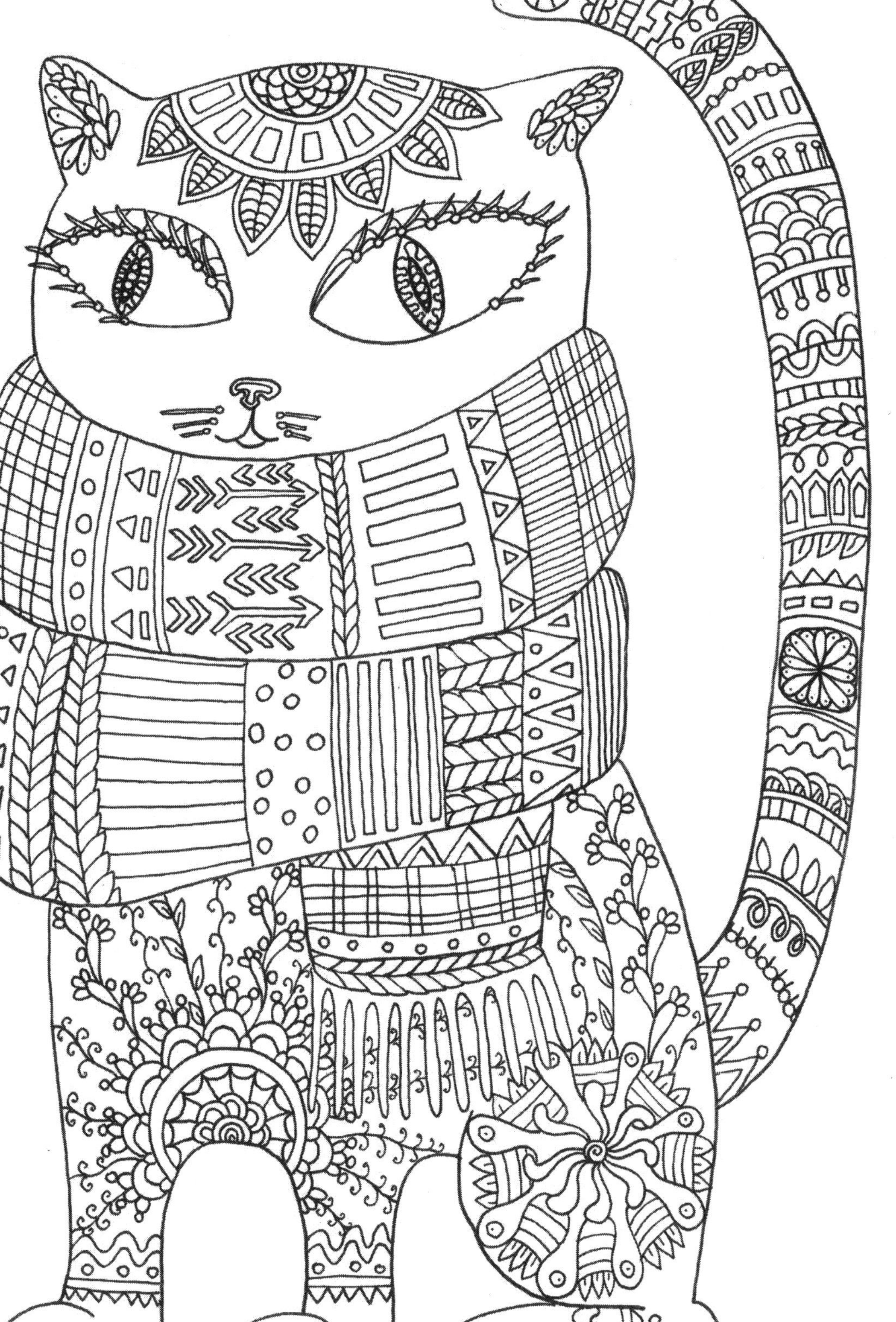

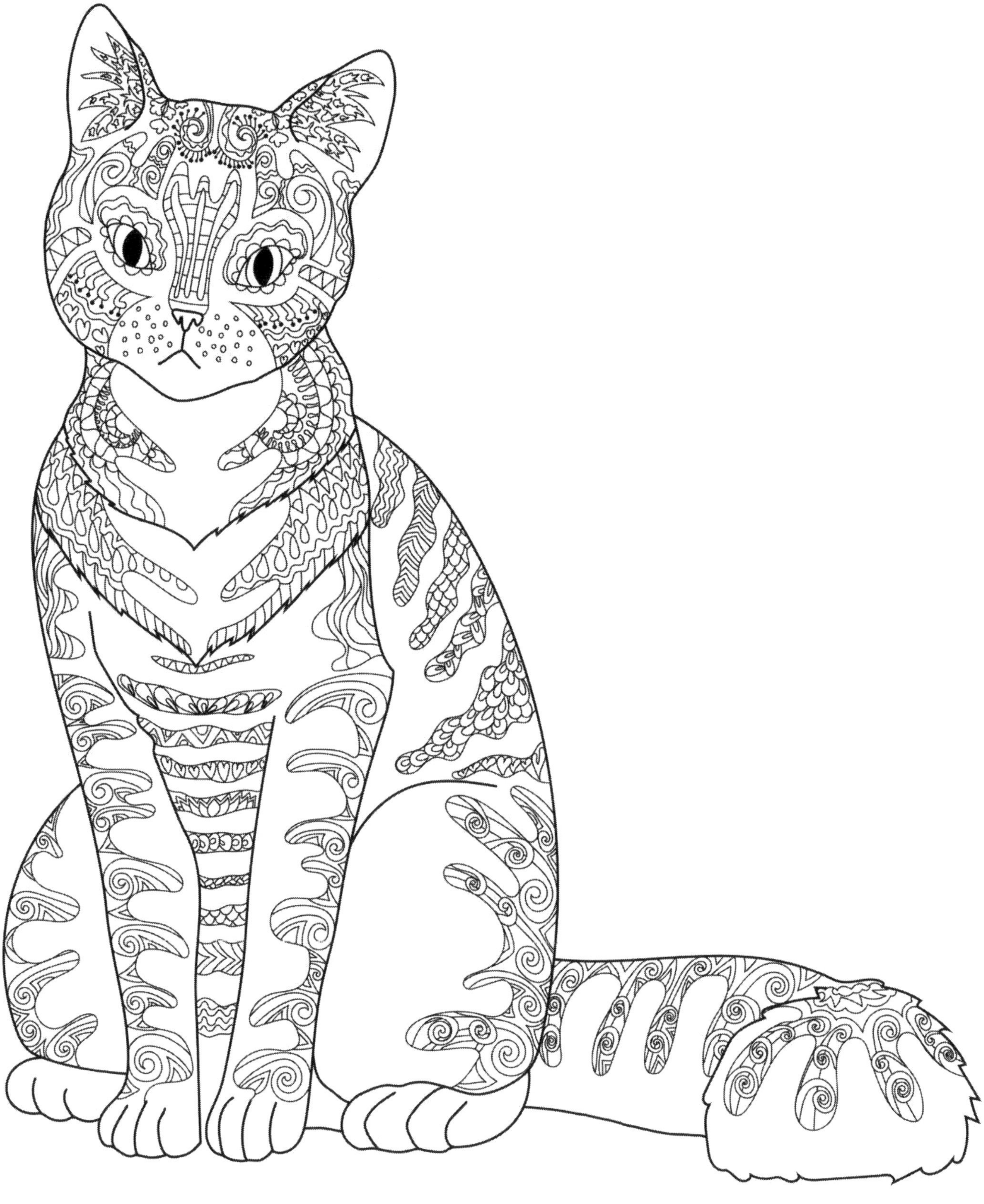

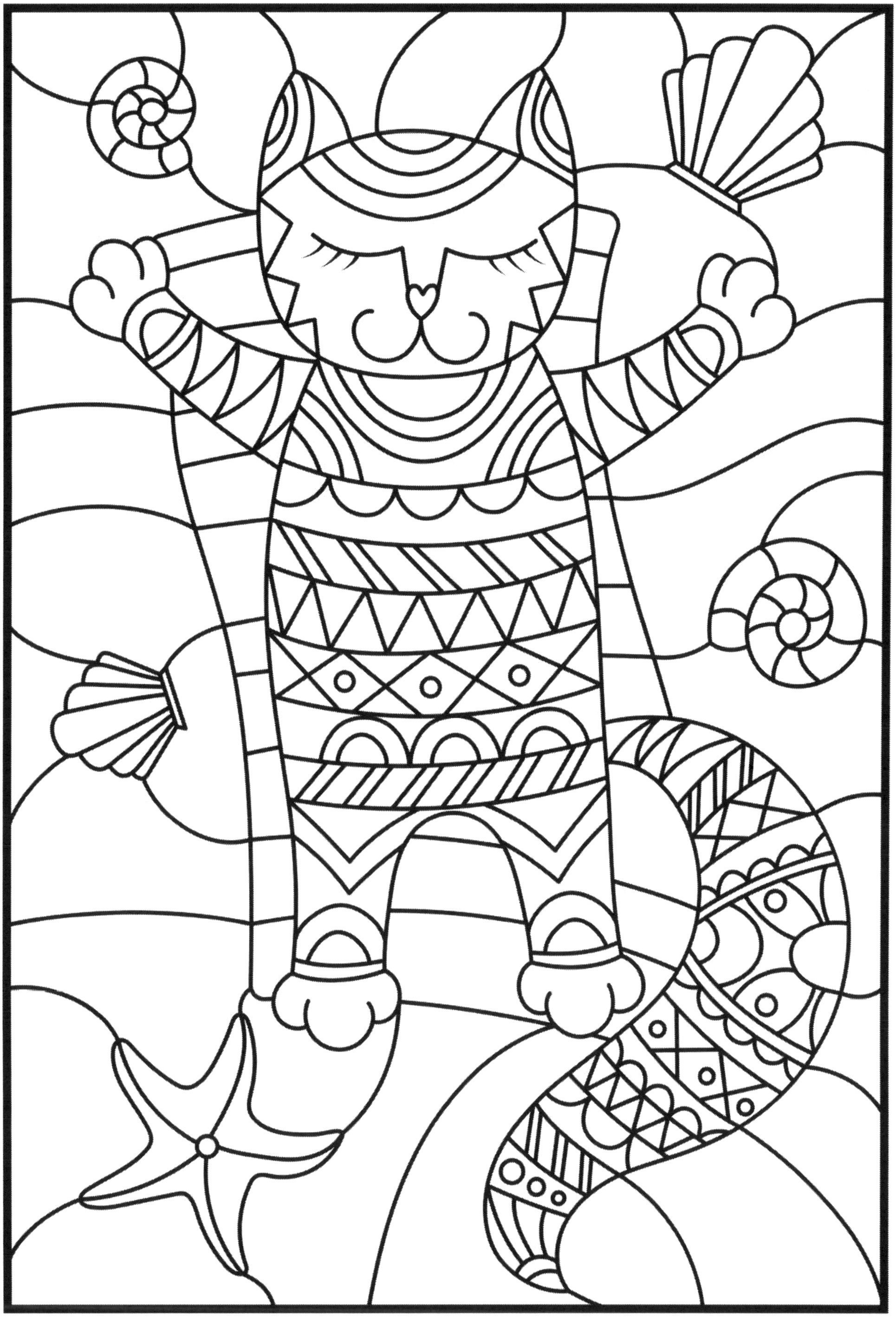

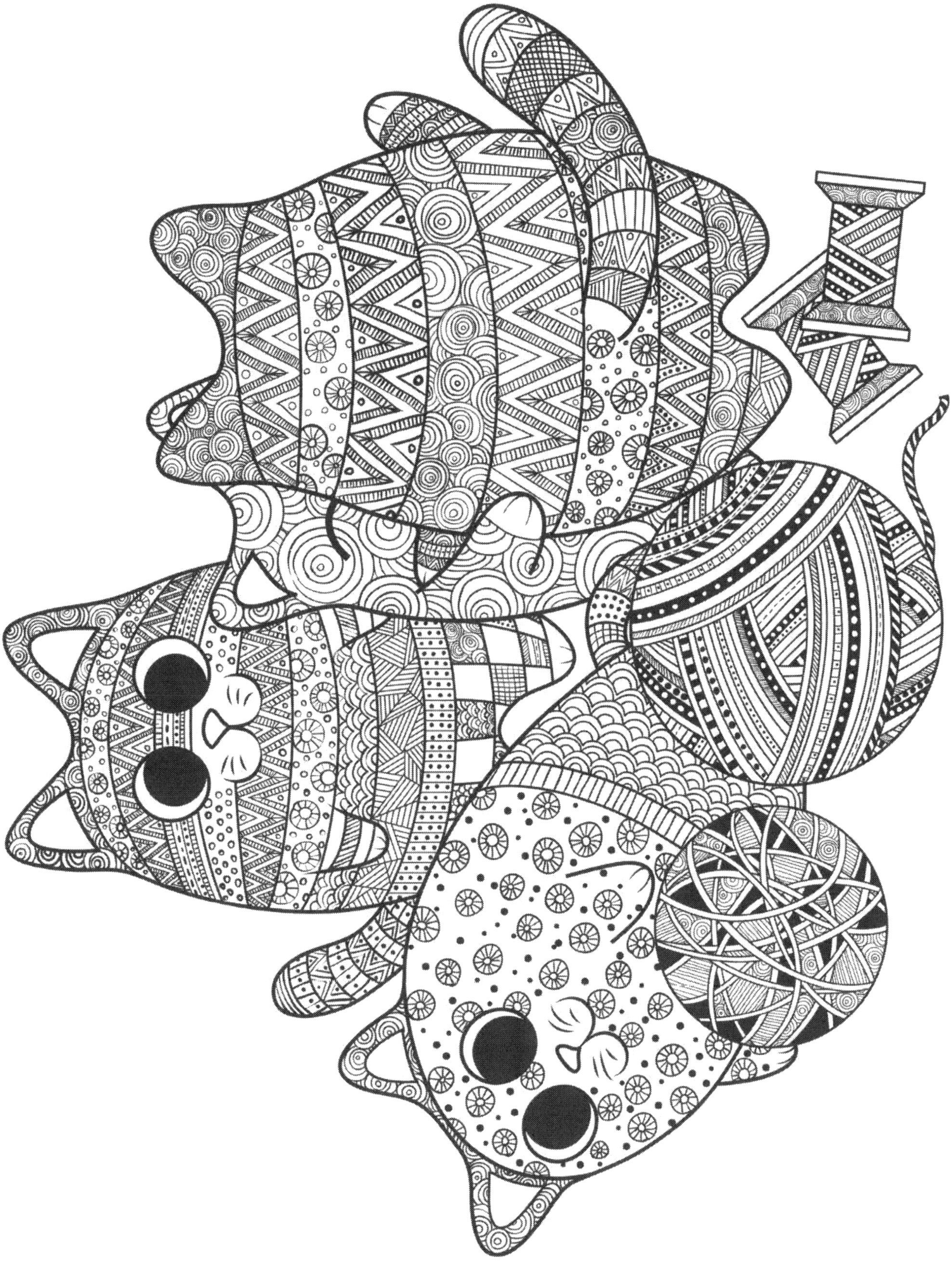

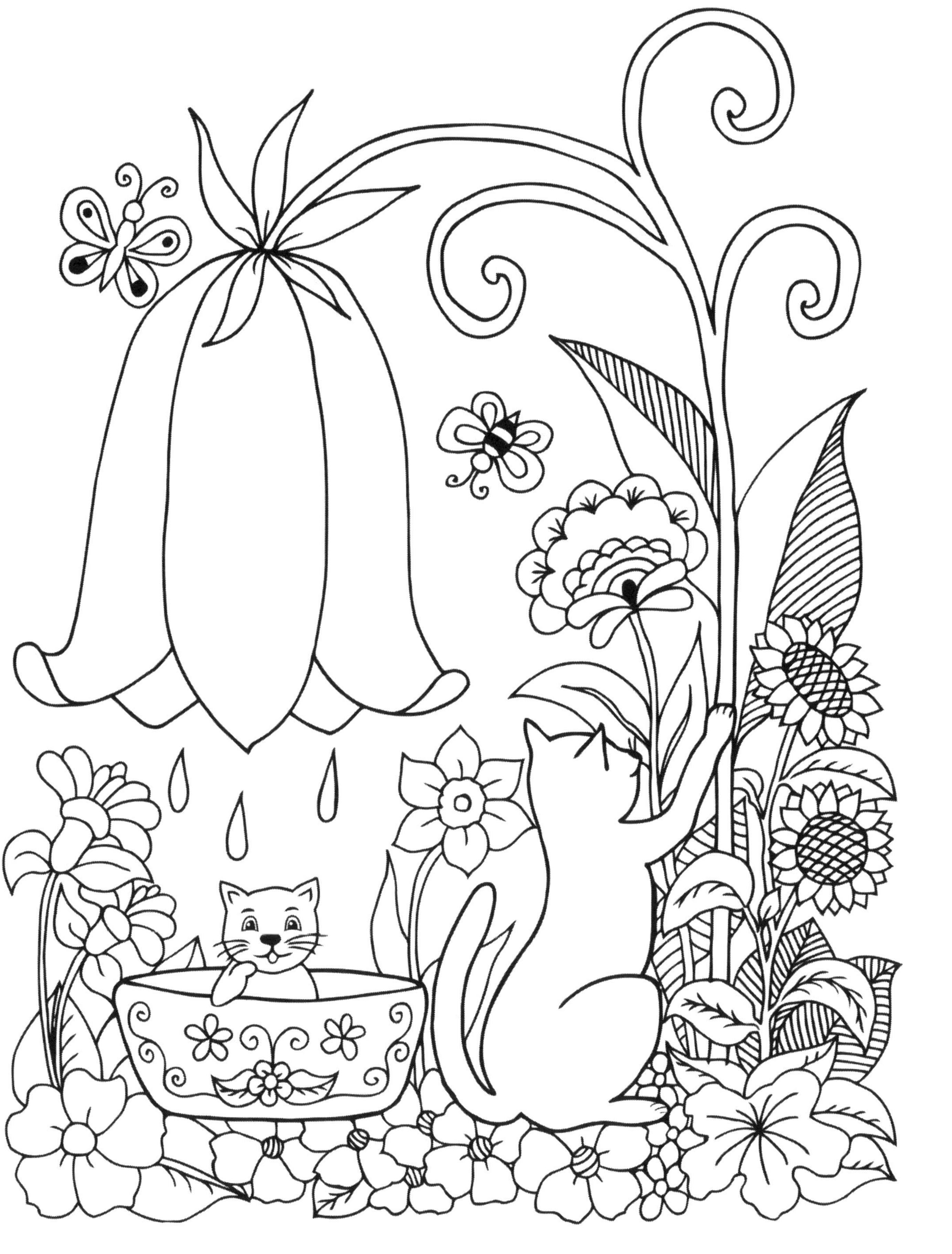

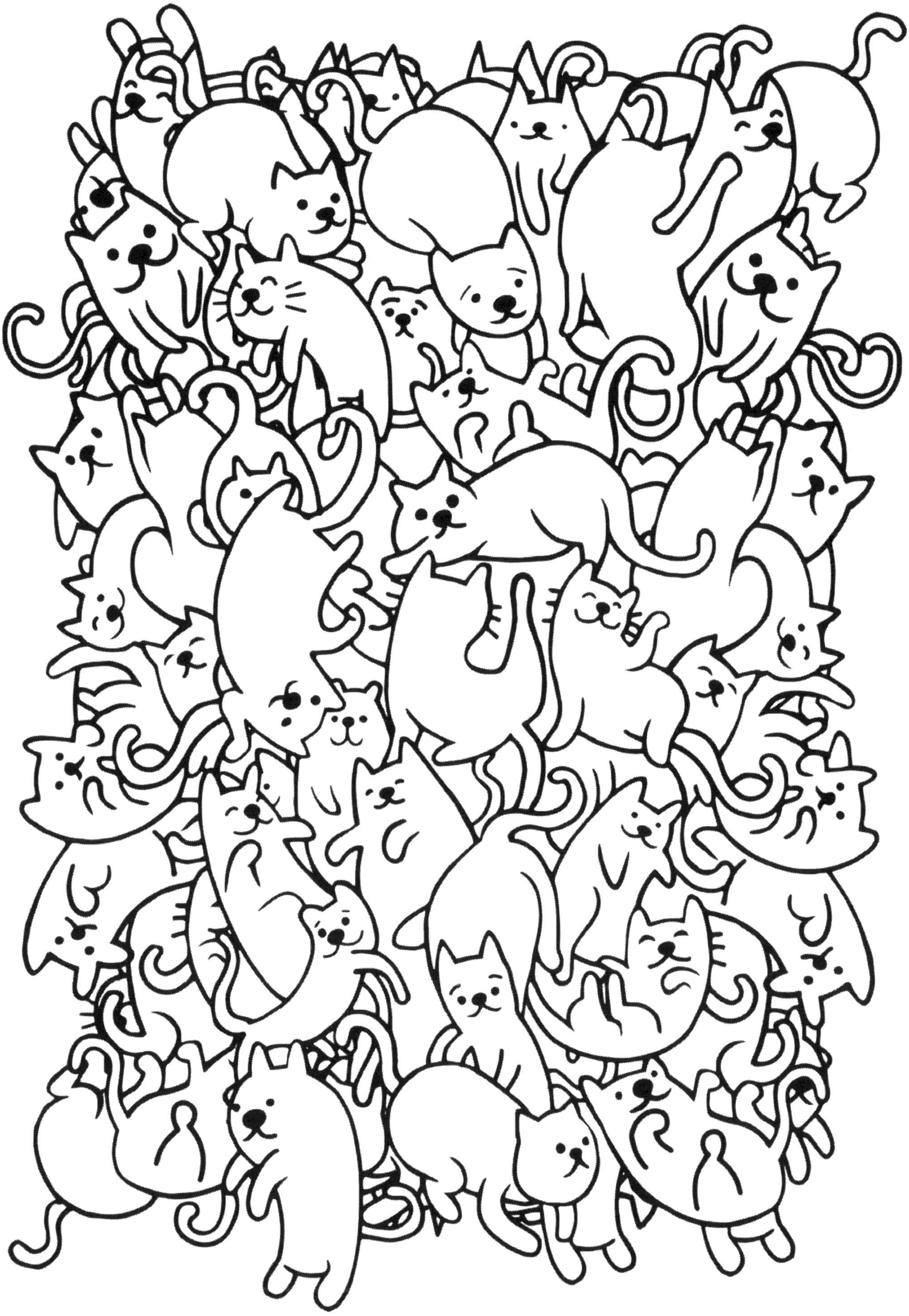

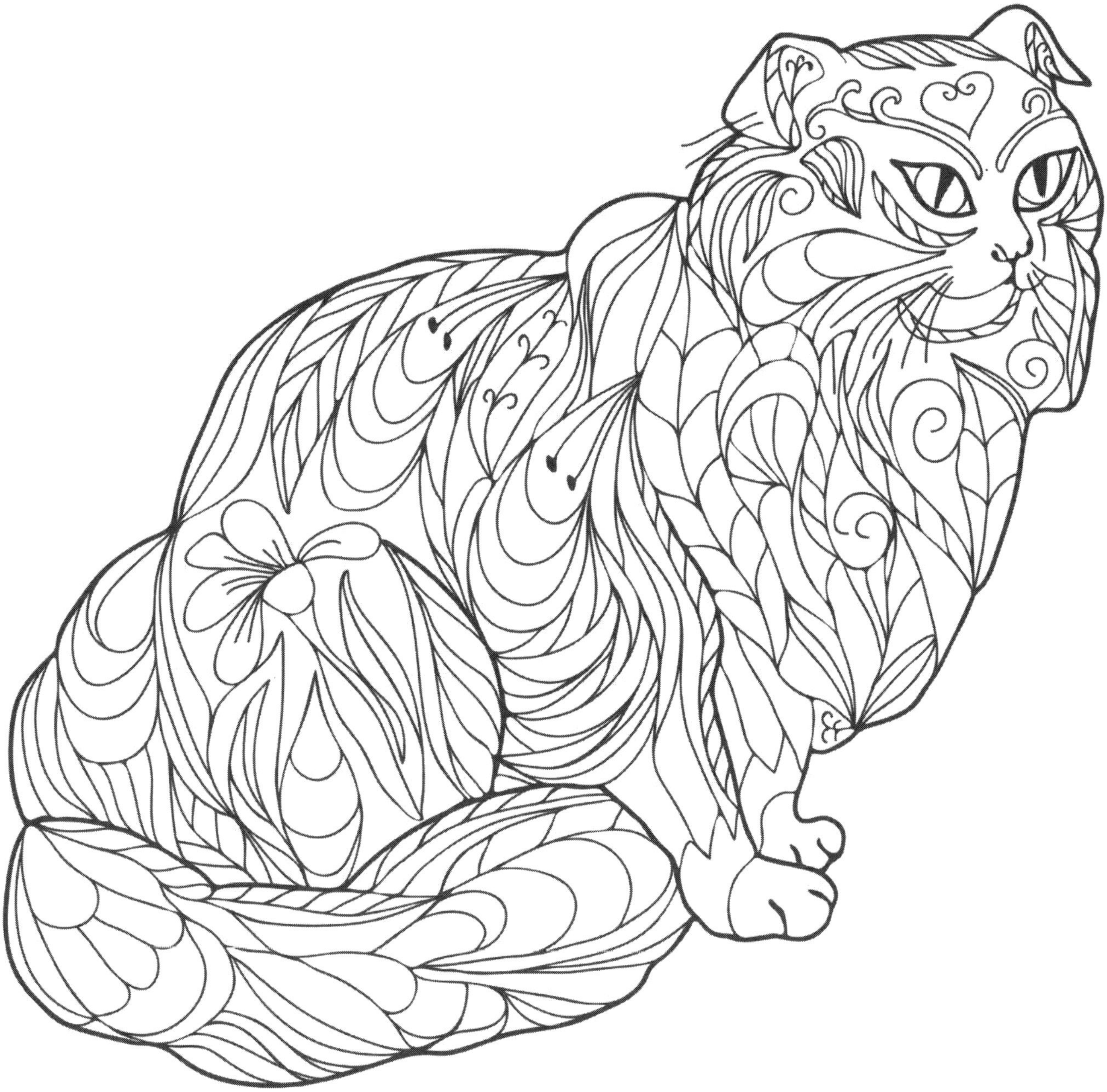

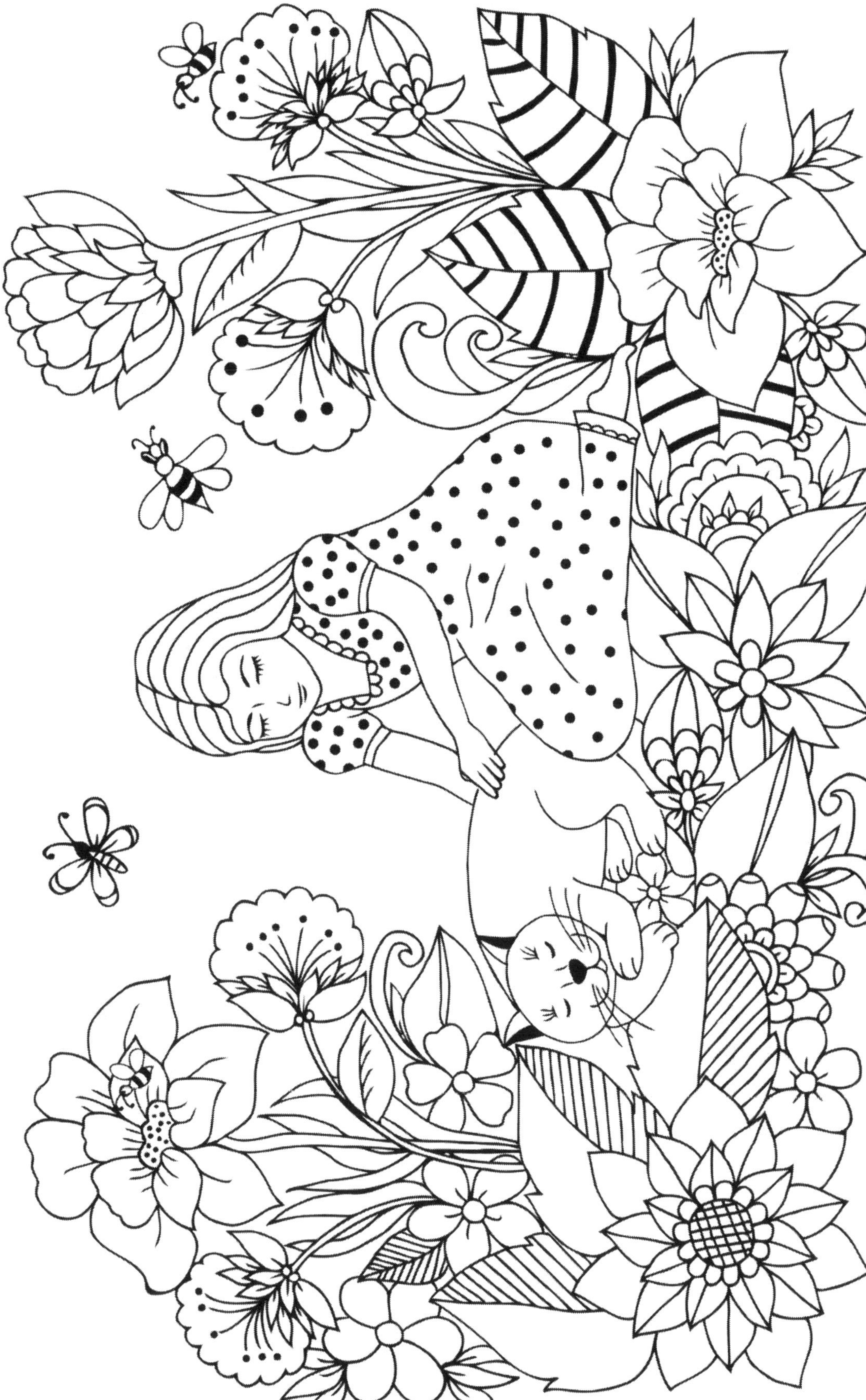

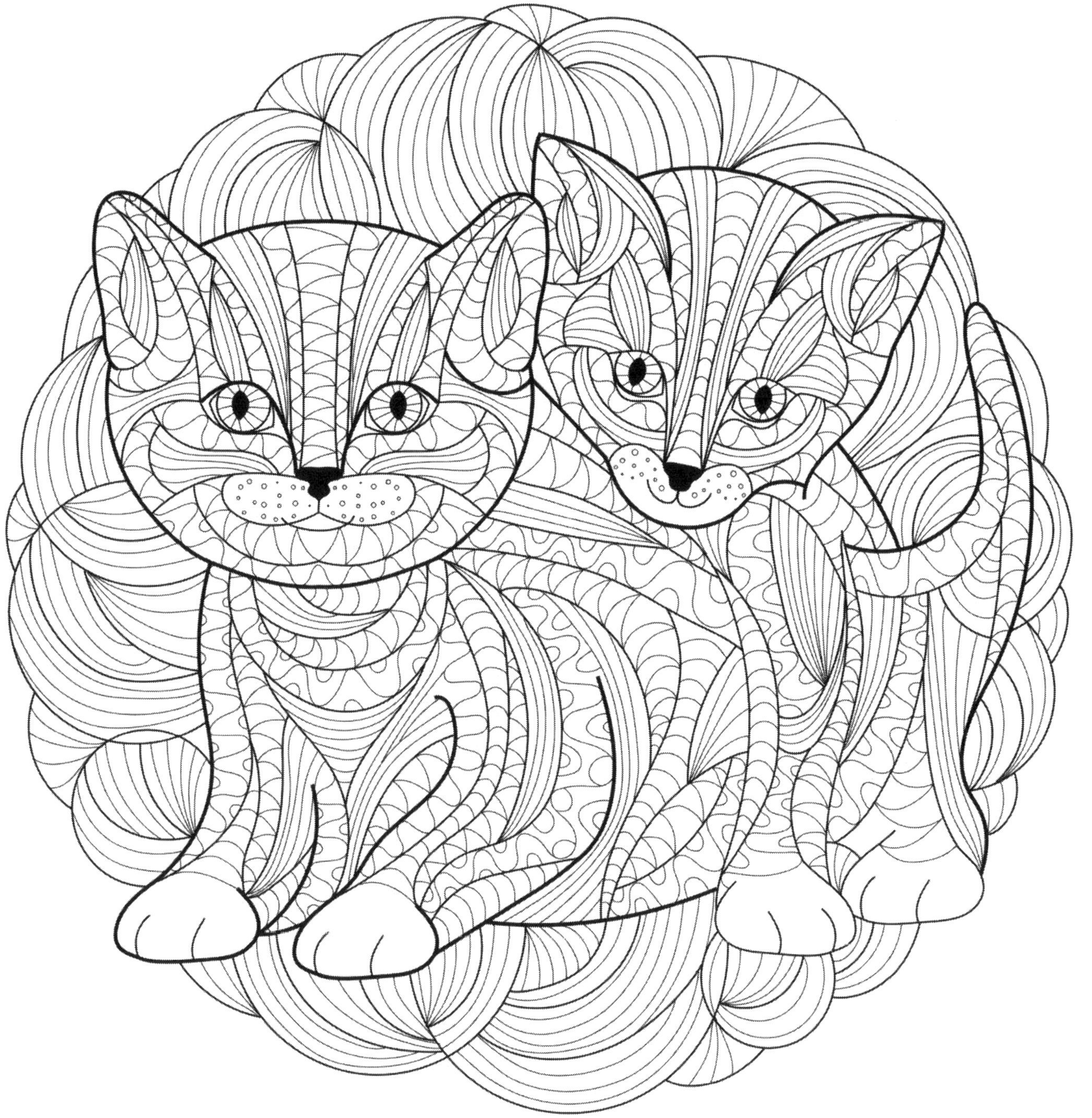

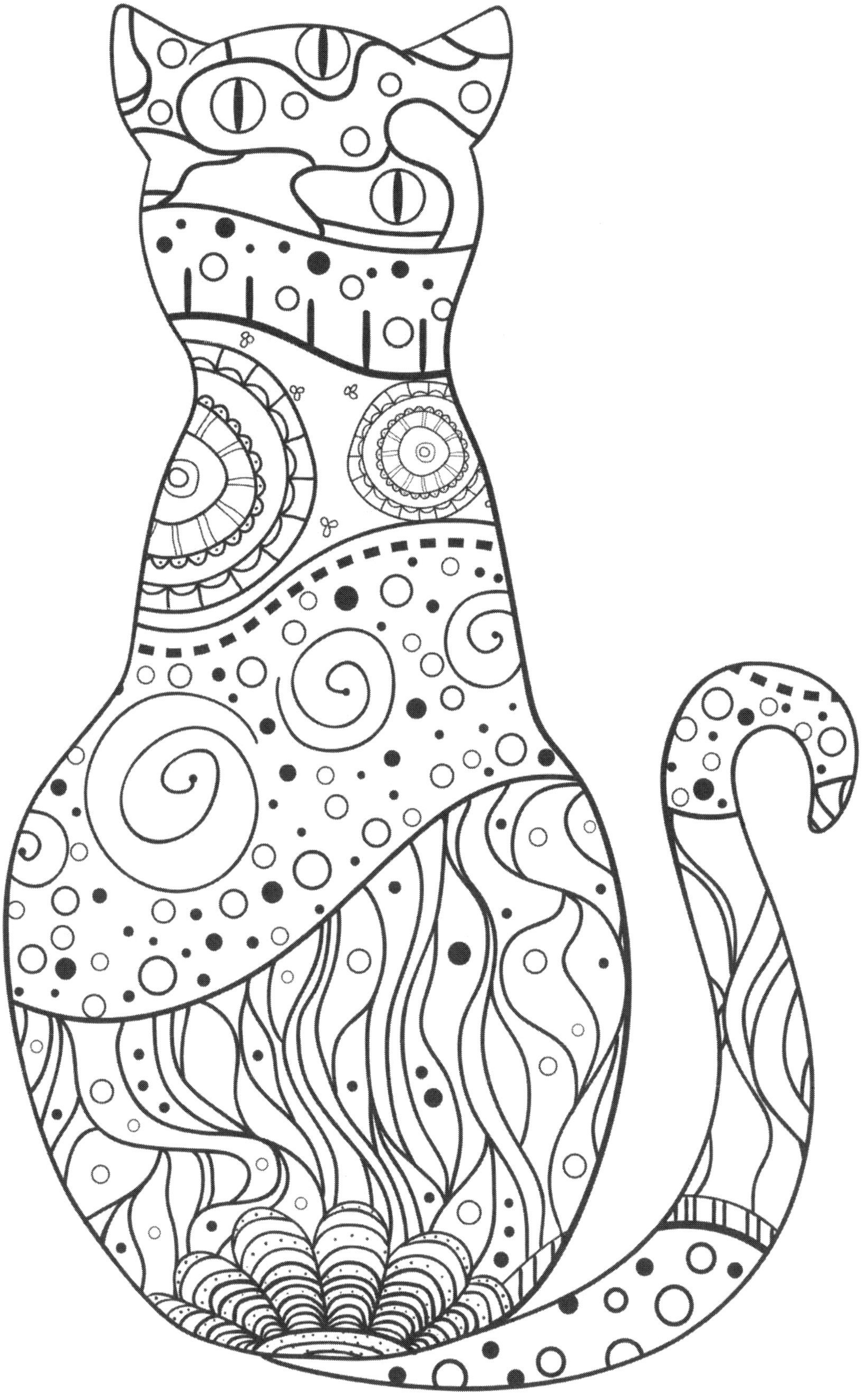

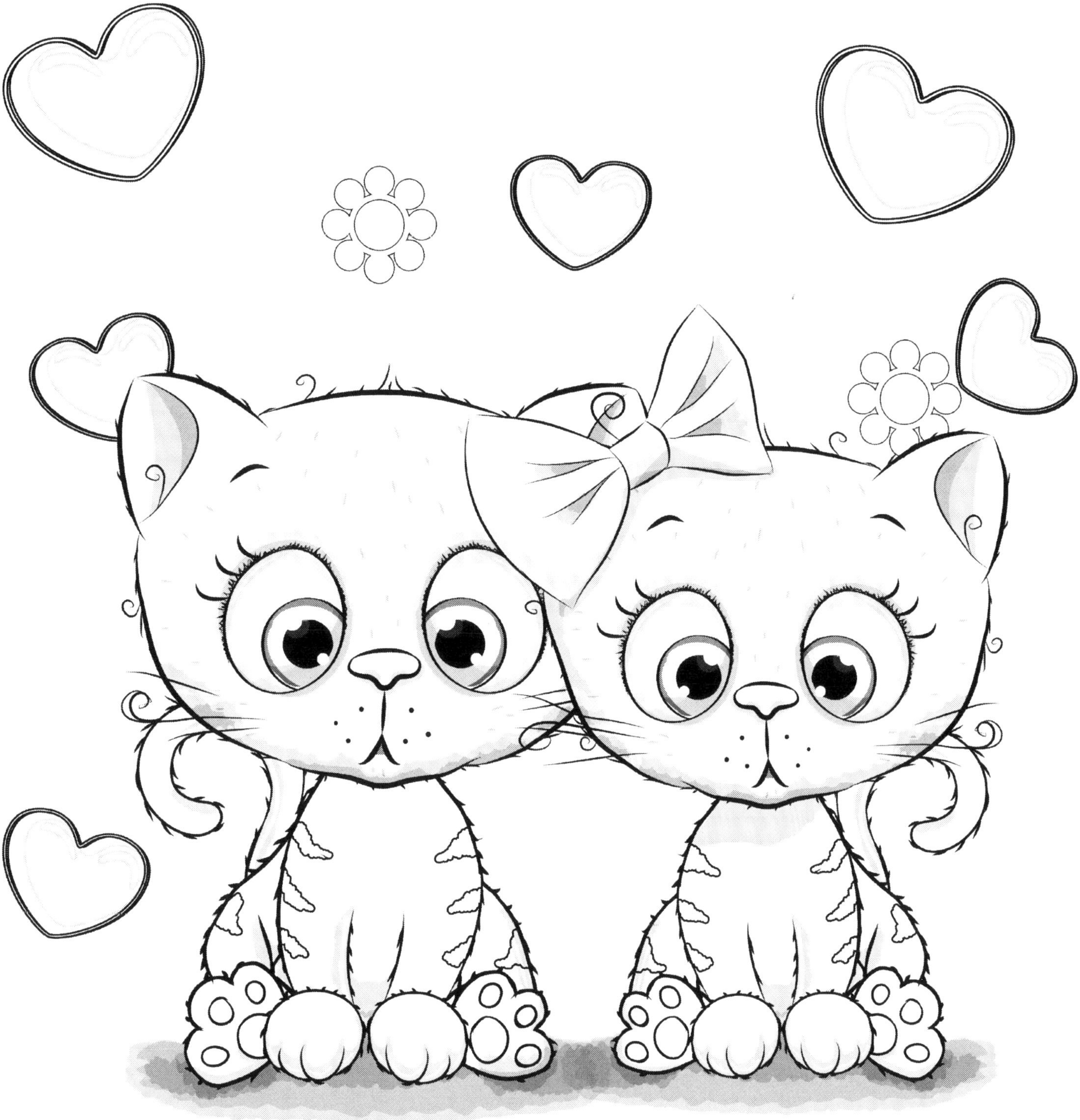

51202965R00033

Made in the USA
Middletown, DE
01 July 2019